M000211199

Divination

· ❯❮ ·

A LITTLE INTRODUCTION TO TAROT, RUNES, TEA LEAVES, AND MORE

Ivy O'Neil

ILLUSTRATED *by*
Sheyda Sabetian

RP MINIS

PHILADELPHIA

RP Minis®
Hachette Book Group
1290 Avenue of the Americas, New York, NY 10104
www.runningpress.com
@Running_Press

Printed in China

First Edition: September 2021

Published by RP Minis, an imprint of Perseus Books, LLC, a subsidiary of Hachette Book Group, Inc. The RP Minis name and logo is a registered trademark of the Hachette Book Group.

The Hachette Speakers Bureau provides a wide range of authors for speaking events. To find out more, go to www.hachettespeakersbureau.com or call (866) 376-6591.

The publisher is not responsible for websites (or their content) that are not owned by the publisher.

Library of Congress Control Number: 2021933055

ISBN: 978-0-7624-7329-8

LREX

10 9 8 7 6 5 4 3 2 1

CONTENTS

*

Introduction

✦

EVERYONE WANTS to know the future, in some way or another. From curiosity about what your workday will look like tomorrow, to wondering if a cute person likes you back, life is full of unanswered questions, and throughout time humans have come up with ways to answer those questions.

Divination, the art of seeing into the future, has been with humanity as long as we've had the awareness that tomorrow will be different from today. People have come up with complex methods of fortunetelling all over the world. Some of them have stayed popular for centuries, and some have almost been forgotten, but the questions people ask hardly change at all. "Will I find

love?" "How can I become rich?"
"Where am I headed in life?"
"How can I help my loved ones?"
Although how we answer questions like this might be different,
the asking itself unites us all.

In this book, you'll learn
about five major forms of
divination that have endured
throughout time. Some of them
might fascinate you, some may
not hold your attention at all, but

I encourage you to give each a try and see how it feels. This book is but a short introduction, and all of these approaches have hundreds of books written on them. If you find one, or all of them, calling to you, I encourage you to keep studying and learning. The wonderful thing about divination, or any magical art, is that you never stop being a student.

Tarot

TAROT MIGHT be the most iconic form of divination. If you've ever been to a psychic, or seen a fortuneteller portrayed on film or TV, they probably used a tarot deck. Tarot is broad, yet specific. It can be used as a tool for meditation and magic, or as party trick with your friends. The wide range of problems, emotions, and scenarios covered in the 78-card deck makes it a perfect aid to turn to for nearly any question. Not for those who wish to keep the future a mystery, the accuracy of the tarot has been called "scary" by many. Whether you want to use tarot in a serious or fun manner, I'm going to lead you through a simple introduction to this storied tool, and you'll be reading cards in no time.

HISTORY

The history of the tarot is as mysterious and complicated as the deck itself. No one can be quite sure when the first deck was created. This has led to many rumors and legends surrounding the tarot. Some say it is from the mythological *Book of Thoth*, by the Egyptian god of magic, while others believe the Devil himself invented the cards.

As far as we know, the first tarot decks appeared in Italy in the fifteenth century. These decks were elaborate expansions of the standard playing-card deck, hand painted by artists, and usually given as gifts to members of Italy's ruling class.

Tarot slowly spread across Europe throughout the Middle Ages, but it wasn't until the arrival of the printing press that its popularity really took off. The first widely distributed tarot deck came from France and is known as The Marseille Tarot. This deck is a favorite with many readers to this day.

In nineteenth-century England, the occult was experiencing a revival. Magic was becoming more popular, and people were beginning to take a new interest in ancient history. Arthur Waite, a member of the Golden Dawn, one of the largest occult societies in England, commissioned a redesign of the famous Marseille Tarot. He hired fellow occultist and artist Pamela Colman Smith to paint the now iconic Rider-Waite-Smith tarot deck. Between

the popularity of this deck, and the many spin-offs, homages, and parodies it has inspired, one could argue that Smith is one of the most influential, and unsung, artists of the last century.

THE MAJOR ARCANA

The tarot is split into two main parts, the Major Arcana and the Minor Arcana. "Arcana" means "mystery," and the two sections roughly correspond to the meanings, messages, and lessons taught by different parts of the tarot. The Major Arcana is filled with big names and concepts, while the Minor is split into suits that correspond to the suits of a deck of playing cards (more on that later, see page 31). Think of it like this: The Major Arcana is big events and concepts that might span great lengths of time and can represent important lessons you need to learn, whereas the Minor Arcana is smaller problems and events, the day-to-day ups and downs we all have to deal with.

With all that in mind, let's dive into some quick definitions for the Major Arcana!

0. THE FOOL: Beginnings and new journeys. You are taking the first step on a bigger path. Are you getting off on the right foot? How do you see yourself: as the main hero or villain of your own story?

1. THE MAGICIAN: Mastery and control. A person who is at the height of their spiritual power. Alternately, someone whose power is based on lies and trickery.

2. THE HIGH PRIESTESS: Intuition and self-knowledge. Your power comes from within. Trust your gut.

3. THE EMPRESS: Feminine power and authority. Creation, whether through literal birth or artistic/intellectual endeavors. Power with others, not over others.

4. THE EMPEROR: Masculine power and authority. Being your own boss and ruler. Alternately, it's lonely at the top. Being in control but having no one to share your kingdom with.

5. THE HIEROPHANT: Knowledge that comes from structured learning and authority figures. Relationships with those in power. Consider learning from those with credentials.

6. THE LOVERS: Love blessed by the universe. Differences coming together to make something new. A relationship's destiny is out of your hands.

7. THE CHARIOT: Racing forward. Being in the driver's seat of your life and destiny. You are heading in the right direction.

8. STRENGTH: The ability to tame demons, external and internal. Strength that comes from working with problems, not dominating or overpowering them.

9. THE HERMIT: Take time away from the world. It's time to turn inward. Not every problem needs comment or action right now.

10. THE WHEEL OF FORTUNE: Things are out of your control at the moment. Depending on if it's reversed or not, this could mean good or bad luck is on your side.

11. JUSTICE: Things are coming to a head. The right thing must be done even if it is difficult.

12. THE HANGED MAN: You are caught in someone's trap, and it will be difficult to get out. Feeling stuck or trapped by circumstance.

13. DEATH: An ending, finality. A new door opens only when another one has been closed. Allow change to transform you.

14. TEMPERANCE: Have patience with yourself as you grow and change. Balance in all things. Your goal is still a long way off.

15. THE DEVIL: Pleasure that comes from the physical world. It's okay, good even, to enjoy yourself, but beware of excess and addiction. Becoming a slave to your desires.

16. THE TOWER: Oof, the worst card in the deck. Calamity and destruction. Difficult truths come to light. Stable foundations are revealed to be made of sand. Revelations that bring both knowledge and pain.

17. THE STAR: Hope, especially after difficult times. The sky clears after the storm, and you are able to see a way forward.

18. THE MOON: Uncharted territory, a dangerous path. Watch your step and trust no one, things are not as they seem.

19. THE SUN: Truth and illumination. Unlike the Tower, this truth brings joy instead of pain. You are seeing things clearly and can take things at face value. Nothing is hidden.

20. JUDGMENT: If you are going to say or do something, do it now; you won't get another chance. Take stock of a situation and see what must stay and what must go.

21. THE WORLD: Completion and finality. This is the end of the journey, accept that everything around you is how it's supposed to be. Peace that comes from reaching the end.

THE MINOR ARCANA
THE SUITS

The Minor Arcana of the tarot is divided into four suits: Cups, Wands, Swords, and Pentacles/ Coins. Each suit relates to a different element and aspect of life.

CUPS: Water, emotions
WANDS: Fire, labor
SWORDS: Air, the mind
PENTACLES: Earth, money

Knowing this helps you get to the root of a problem much faster. For instance, if you ask the tarot a question about love, but get mostly Pentacles in your reading, your problem might not really be about feelings or romance, but about money and resources. With that in mind, let's dive into the Minor Arcana!

CUPS

ACE OF CUPS: Emotional fulfilment. Your cup runs over with good things.

TWO OF CUPS: A relationship. Specifically, built on mutual trust and respect.

THREE OF CUPS: A gathering of friends. Coming together with others for a common purpose.

FOUR OF CUPS: Depression. You are being given a gift, but cannot see it.

FIVE OF CUPS: A terrible thing happened, yes, but you are spending too much time looking at what you don't have, and not enough looking at what you do have. All is not lost.

SIX OF CUPS: Dreams of childhood. Return to your roots for answers.

SEVEN OF CUPS: Overwhelmed with false choices. Be discerning.

EIGHT OF CUPS: It's okay to walk away when things get hard.

NINE OF CUPS: Joy from material goods that won't last if hoarded. Happiness is only real when shared.

TEN OF CUPS: A happy family. The completion of an emotional journey. Returning home.

PAGE OF CUPS: This person is not what they seem. Expect surprises.

KNIGHT OF CUPS: Setting off on a journey. A quest for a romantic or artistic goal.

QUEEN OF CUPS: A clever woman, someone who can see their emotions objectively.

KING OF CUPS: A lover. Depending on the placement in your reading, a man who is either very kind or very cruel to women.

WANDS

ACE OF WANDS: The start of new work or projects.

TWO OF WANDS: Your needs conflict with the needs of others. Find ways to compromise.

THREE OF WANDS: Patience. The outcome is unknown. You should prepare for what you want to happen.

FOUR OF WANDS: Traditionally, a marriage. Can also mean collaboration, especially at work or creative projects.

FIVE OF WANDS: Petty conflict. Drama, ego, and arguments over nothing. Try to stay out of it.

SIX OF WANDS: Victory! Allow yourself to rejoice, it's okay to show off your accomplishments.

SEVEN OF WANDS: Deep seated conflict. Enemies all around. You are in a fight for survival, good luck!

EIGHT OF WANDS: Unexpected, rapid change. Chaos will reign, but only momentarily.

NINE OF WANDS: Keeping it together, but just barely. Anxiety over knowing things could come crashing down at any moment.

TEN OF WANDS: You may feel overwhelmed by work and can't see the way home, but you are so close! Don't give up yet!

PAGE OF WANDS: An animated, passionate young person. Someone who excites and inspires you.

KNIGHT OF WANDS: Movement, change. Can be a literal move or relaxation.

QUEEN OF WANDS: Someone who is comfortable with chaos, change, and uncertainty. Meeting transformation with peace of mind.

KING OF WANDS: A boss or person in charge at a work environment. Someone who feels comfortable in charge.

SWORDS

ACE OF SWORDS: A flash of inspiration, a shock of courage. Your mind and will are strong.

TWO OF SWORDS: A choice must be made. Do not make it lightly as it will have great consequence, however you must choose.

THREE OF SWORDS: Heartbreak, loss, pain. Nothing happy to say about this card!

FOUR OF SWORDS: Retreat from the world and rest for a short time, even a weekend. Take time to relax.

FIVE OF SWORDS: You've won, but now is not the time to gloat. Bragging will drive others away in the long run.

SIX OF SWORDS: Difficult times lay ahead, but you will have help. Don't go alone. Reach out to your spirits and ancestors.

SEVEN OF SWORDS: Trickery. Either someone is lying to you, or you are lying to yourself.

EIGHT OF SWORDS: You are trapped in a cage of your own mind and ways of thinking. Things may seem impossible, but a change in mindset gives you freedom.

NINE OF SWORDS: Anxiety, fear, worry that keeps you up at night. Things will be bad for now.

TEN OF SWORDS: The final, gruesome end of a challenging time. The sun will rise again someday, but for now, the hurt from what has happened lingers.

PAGE OF SWORDS: A worried figure, someone unsure of themselves and their power.

KNIGHT OF SWORDS: Unexpected news. Believe in your vision and make it happen.

QUEEN OF SWORDS: A strong, smart woman who welcomes a challenge. Don't back down.

KING OF SWORDS: A figure who is clear and calm in their opinions and beliefs. Don't feel the need to prove yourself to others.

PENTACLES

ACE OF PENTACLES: A new job or avenue of making money. Seize opportunities!

TWO OF PENTACLES: Juggling a lot of projects and aspects of life. You might be too busy.

THREE OF PENTACLES: You are working hard and being recognized for it.

FOUR OF PENTACLES: Stubbornness. Don't think that what you currently have is all there is in life.

FIVE OF PENTACLES: Poverty, desperation. Relief from pain is just around the corner.

SIX OF PENTACLES: Do not be stingy, but do not over-give of yourself. Have healthy boundaries around helping others.

SEVEN OF PENTACLES: Impatience. You have planted the seeds of success, and now you must wait for them to grow.

EIGHT OF PENTACLES: Hard but enjoyable work. Finding joy in the task at hand.

NINE OF PENTACLES: Enjoy the fruits of your labor. Treat yourself!

TEN OF PENTACLES: A sudden inheritance or unexpected influx of cash or resources.

PAGE OF PENTACLES: A student or novice. Someone excited to learn and develop their goals.

KNIGHT OF PENTACLES: An entrepreneur or person with a cherished idea. Be careful and deliberate with where you put your efforts.

QUEEN OF PENTACLES: A person who is well attuned to their surroundings and the needs of their community.

KING OF PENTACLES: Making money from money. Wealth and security that comes easily and sustains itself.

A SIMPLE SPREAD

To get started learning tarot, the easiest thing you can do is a "card for the day" pull. Every morning, while you are getting ready for your day, take a moment to close your eyes, shuffle your deck, and ask the cards what the world has in store for you that day. Simply pull one card, and spend some time thinking about it. Throughout your day, see if any themes from the card come up.

Past-Present-Future

Another simple option is a "past, present, future" reading. Think of an issue or question while you shuffle.

Pull three cards:

The first for the past.

The second for the present.

The third for the future.

This will help you gain insight on where an issue started, what is happening now, and what is likely to happen in the future.

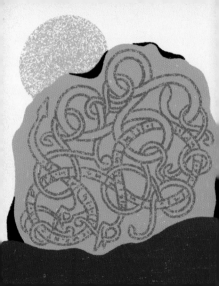

The Runes

LESS POPULAR than tarot, but no less powerful, are the runes. Runes are the pictographic alphabet and divination system that ancient Scandinavians and other Northern Europeans used from around 200 BC up through much of the Middle Ages.

The runes can be used for spells and magic, but for now we are going to stick to their use as tools for divination. If this chapter inspires you, remember you can always make your own runes by drawing the symbols on rocks or pieces of wood!

HISTORY AND MYTHOLOGY

In Norse Mythology, the runes were something like the Matrix, the secret code that controlled reality. Odin, the god of wisdom and king of the Aesir clan of gods and spirits, was said to have hung himself from the tree of life, Yggdrasil, for nine days and nights in order to learn the runes' secrets. He suffered greatly, and even lost an eye in the process! Fortunately, we don't need to go to such great lengths to learn a bit about the runes.

Runes made up a big part of Scandinavian society, showing up in everything from art and carvings to jewelry and architecture. Runes were believed to have power all on their own, but when combined with other runes, people could weave "sigils" or spells in picture form. In places like Iceland, this grew into a complex magical artform. To this day, runestones dot the landscape of Scandinavia, binding spirits in place and telling stories of the distant past.

THE TYPES OF RUNES

Like any language, runes evolved over time. There are three main types of runes one can use, each coming from different places and time periods.

THE ELDER FUTHARK is the oldest and most popular system of runes, and the one we'll be looking at here. It was developed and used in Sweden between the second and eighth centuries.

ANGLO SAXON RUNES are slightly more complicated than the Elder Futhark. They were popular in England and the British Isles from the fifth to eleventh century.

THE YOUNGER FUTHARK is the most simplified form of runes. It was developed as people were becoming exposed to the Roman alphabet and the runes were changing into modern letters. It was developed in southern Scandinavia between the ninth and eleventh centuries.

A LIST OF RUNES
& THEIR DEFINITIONS

All runes have a literal meaning and a divinatory meaning. These meanings reflect the world the runes emerged into and the values of ancient Scandinavian society, similar to many Asian languages and characters today. Some runes might look familiar because they became letters in the English alphabet!

ᛗ ᛊ

ᚠ Fehu * CATTLE
Wealth, conflict that comes from
wealth. Make a donation or share
the wealth.

ᚢ Uruz * OX, RAIN
Strength to face any obstacle.

ᚦ Thurisaz * GIANT, THORN
Danger, particularly dangerous for
women. Run away!

ᚨ Ansuz * GOD, ODIN
Messages, look out for signs.

R **Raido** * RIDE, JOURNEY
You are on the right path, enjoy
the journey.

< **Kenaz** * FIRE
Keep a positive attitude, time to
step into your power.

X **Gebo** * GIFT
Good things, a wonderful gift.

P **Wunjo** * JOY
Inner peace, rest after battle.

ᚺ Hagalaz * HAIL
Upheaval, sudden endings,
new beginnings.

ᚾ Naudiz * NEED
Exercise restraint, you will lack
resources.

ᛁ Isaz * ICE
Immobility, be patient and wait for
circumstances to change.

ᛃ Jera * YEAR
Time heals all wounds, the pain
you're feeling will pass with time.

ᚨ

Eihwaz ＊ YEW TREE
Strength, endurance, stand your
ground and don't back down.

Pertho ＊ GAME, CHANCE
Fate and destiny are at play, however, it is a destiny you can change.

Algiz ＊ PROTECTION
You are being protected by the
gods, spirits, or people in positions
of power.

ξ **Sowilo** * SUN, HOPE
Have hope, victory will soon be
yours, and whatever hardships you
are facing will end.

$\uparrow$ **Tiwaz** * THE GOD OF WAR
Stay focused and stay on the path.

B **Berkanan** * BIRCH TREE, BEAUTY
Time to enjoy life and beautify your
space. Treat yourself!

M **Ehwaz** * HORSE
Movement, change. Get ready for
change, internally or externally.

ᛗ Mannaz ✳ HUMANS, HUMANKIND
It is time for self-reflection and
humility. Not everything is
about you.

ᛚ Laguz ✳ WATER
Some things in your life might fall
away or fade. It's okay, let them go.

◇ Ingwaz ✳ THE GOD OF FERTILITY
Love, sex, and pleasure are
coming your way. Enjoy yourself!

◊ **Othala** ✳ LAND, INHERITANCE
Remember your roots and where
you come from. An inheritance
might be coming your way.

ᛞ **Dagaz** ✳ DAY
Triumph, clarity, happy endings.

PRESENT

PAST   FUTURE

A Simple Spread

Like in tarot, the easiest ways to learn the runes are simple "rune a day" readings or "past, present, future" readings. Since runes are usually carved onto rocks, wood, or pieces of bone, they work a little differently than cards.

Keep your runes in a pouch or bag. Hold the bag in your hands and concentrate on a question.

Pull one to three runes out from inside
the bag and set them down.

Remember rune meanings can be very
complex. Consider keeping a journal
with what messages from the runes
come up for you, and see how their
meanings map onto your life over time.

Playing Cards

YOU DON'T need fancy tools or expensive decks of cards to perform divination. In fact, throughout history people have used cheap, accessible things as divination tools. This makes them easy to come by, and easy to hide from people whom you might want to keep your magic a secret from. One of the most popular tools of divination in the last few centuries has been the humble pack of playing cards.

HISTORY

Playing cards were first developed in China in the ninth century, and they spread slowly across the globe on the Silk Road. Traders from the Middle East took the Chinese cards and adapted them using their own artwork and culture, adding kings, clubs, swords, and viziers to the deck. This is how four suits and twelve cards to a suit became standardized.

Playing cards eventually made their way from Egypt to Europe around the fourteenth century, and from there the popularity of playing cards grew. Different regions added their own twists on the suits, such as acorns and bells, but it was eventually the French who came up with the spades, hearts, clubs, and diamonds we know today.

As playing cards were easier to find than tarot, they were much more

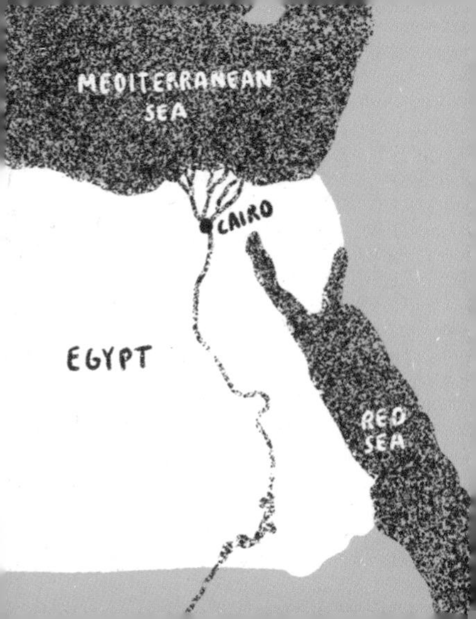

MEDITERRANEAN
SEA
CAIRO
EGYPT
RED
SEA

popular for use in divination. It's when playing cards reached North America that their use for this purpose really took off. Playing cards were incorporated into magical systems like hoodoo and rootwork by African slaves and Black Americans. These systems are rich blends of African, European, and Native American folk magic and religion that remain a part of the complex culture of the American South.

CARD MEANINGS

Since playing cards have been around for centuries, there are many meanings ascribed to different cards. The one chosen usually depends on the region the card reader comes from, particularly in the United States where playing cards are very popular in traditional rootwork and conjure magic. The following list is adapted from my own interpretations, as well as those given in Professor Charles Porterfield's book *A Deck of Spells*. I recommend checking out that book for more great information on playing-card divination!

SPADES

Spades are no fun. They are all about death, pain, and conflict.

ACE: Death, finality, endings

TWO: Duel, conflict

THREE: Loss, tears, depression

FOUR: The sick-bed, tiredness

FIVE: A field of brambles, protect yourself

SIX: A difficult journey ahead

SEVEN: Bad luck

EIGHT: Addiction, alcoholism

NINE: Legal trouble, a sudden ending, an ending that brings peace

TEN: Funeral, a final end, sadness

JACK: A dangerous young man

QUEEN: A cruel, judgmental woman

KING: A dark, cold man or a soldier

DIAMONDS

Diamonds are all about money, wealth, and fun.

ACE: A gift, a letter

TWO: A contract, something you desire will be yours soon, a good arrangement

THREE: Help from another

FOUR: Passionate love, physical attraction

FIVE: Rewards for good choices

SIX: Abundance, streets paved with gold

SEVEN: Good luck, wishes granted, blessings

EIGHT: Unexpected money is coming your way

NINE: Watch the store, protect your money

TEN: A wild party, a short-lived love

JACK: A wily young man

QUEEN: A sex worker, a fair woman, an empowered woman

KING: A dominant man, a wealthy man, a banker

CLUBS

The clubs are all about work and labor.

ACE: A new job, steady work

TWO: A new work partnership, an agreement

THREE: A quarrel, a fight

FOUR: Travel for work, staying at another's house

FIVE: Work, working hard

SIX: Possibly moving, in it for a long time

SEVEN: Overworking yourself, take a break

EIGHT: Be direct about your desires

NINE: Stay the course, protect your assets

TEN: A union, a group of workers, blessings from working together

JACK: A light-hearted young man

QUEEN: A wise, older woman

KING: A strong, severe man

HEARTS

Hearts are all about love and feelings.

ACE: A new love

TWO: Lovers coming together

THREE: A rival in love

FOUR: Romantic love, the home

FIVE: Growth of love over time

SIX: The path to the heart

SEVEN: Fake friends, too much of a good thing

EIGHT: Addicted to love

NINE: Treat yourself, a marriage

TEN: Found family, finally overcoming hardship

JACK: A flirty, fun person

QUEEN: A generous, kind woman; a mother

KING: A fair, patient man; a father

* · · ▰▰▰ · ·

A SIMPLE SPREAD:
YES/NO QUESTIONS

Playing cards are a great tool to use for simple "yes" or "no" questions. Simply ask your question as you shuffle the deck and pull three cards. Red means yes, and black means no. Mixed colors can temper how strong of a yes or no the answer is. For example:

3 Red: Strong yes

2 Red/1 Black: Qualified yes

3 Black: Strong no

2 Black/1 Red: Qualified no

The meanings of the individual cards can also be interpreted for further insight.

Geomancy

WHILE OFTEN overlooked and nearly forgotten today, geomancy was once one of the most popular forms of divination in the world. Translated as "seeing by earth," during the Middle Ages and Renaissance people of all social classes practiced geomancy at least sometimes, even inventing prototypes of computers to perform this particular kind of divination!

Geomancy is divination based on dots marked on a piece of paper or in the dirt. Sounds easy, right? While it's easy, and really fun once you get the hang of it, geomancy can be extremely complicated and a little difficult to learn at first. No worries though, I'm going to walk you through it one step at a time.

Each of the sixteen figures in geomancy correspond to astrological signs, planets, and elements. This means that geomancy can be used for more than just telling the future or giving advice. The symbols can also be used as talismans for magic and spell work.

HISTORY

Geomancy started in the Middle East, most likely Egypt, around the ninth century. As Arabic books of magic spread throughout Europe and were translated, more and more people began to learn geomancy.

Because the performance of geomancy only requires even and odd numbers, it was available to everyone, both educated and not. Queen Elizabeth I's magician John Dee famously used geomancy to help make many important decisions regarding her reign, but it was also embraced by poor and working-class people across Europe and the Middle East.

In the nineteenth century, geomancy regained some popularity with the Golden Dawn and followers of Aleister Crowley, but

since it is a form of divination
that takes some time to preform,
it has never quite gained traction
in our modern, fast-paced world.

HOW-TO:
WITH PLAYING CARDS OR DICE

Geomancy is about making a series of four-rowed figures based on even and odd numbers, and refining those numbers until you have a symbol that gives you your answer.

To perform geomancy, you need a paper, pen, and something that will give you even and odd numbers. This can be literally any-thing—the cracks on the sidewalk, the leaves on a branch—but for simplicity I recommend a deck of playing cards or dice.

To make a geomantic figure, roll a die four times and mark whether the number that comes up is even or odd, with two dots for even, and one for odd. Arrange these in a vertical row, and voila! You have made a geomantic figure!

You can stop there for a quick answer to a question, but to do a real geomancy reading, you will need to perform this action a few more times. Below is what's called a "shield chart." There are other charts you can make that map onto astrological charts, but we're going to keep things simple for now. Let's go through it and make a chart as we go!

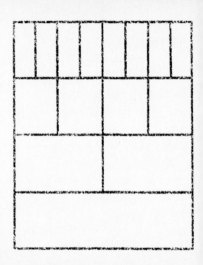

Take a blank piece of paper and make four horizontal lines. Divide the first row into eight boxes, the second into four, the third into two, and leave the last one as is. Like we learned above, take your die or pack of cards, and make eight figures, one for each box on the top row.

Begin to refine the symbols down by adding up the dots. Take two adjacent symbols and add up the dots row by row. If the amount is now even, make two dots, if the amount is now odd, make one, and so on. Mark the new symbol in the box beneath the two symbols from which you derived it. Repeat this step for the next two rows. See how above you're blending symbols together until eventually it all refines down to one?

You can take the bottom row as your general "answer," but for a fuller picture, you should look at the bottom three boxes and interpret the symbols there.

Each figure in geomancy corresponds to different elements, qualities, and ideas (see page 111). If the two "witnesses," or the figures in the second to last row, and the "judge" in the bottom row all have positive or affirming meanings, congratulations! You have reached a definite "yes" or affirmative answer to your question. If the judge and witnesses all have negative connotations, that's a definite "no." If the witnesses are negative, but the judge positive, you will have victory after a lot of struggle. And if the witnesses are positive, but the judge negative, you will have success, but it will be short-lived.

It's a complicated, yet accessible system of divination. Once you get the hang of it though, geomancy is addicting. Try it when you are bored at school, when you are with friends, or when you just want to practice your basic arithmetic skills!

SYMBOL DEFINITIONS

PUER: Boy, a warrior, a fiery spirit, Aries, Fire

AMISSIO: Loss, doing without, negative outcome, Taurus, Earth

ALBUS: White, wisdom, spiritual growth and healing, Gemini, Air

POPULUS: The people, family, friends, community, Cancer, Water

FORTUNA MAJOR: Great fortune, celebration, prosperity, Leo, Fire

CONJUNCTIO: Union, friendship, love, marriage, partnerships, Virgo, Earth

PUELLA: Girl, cleanliness, beauty, precision, Libra, Air

RUBEUS: Red, passion, arguments, conflict, Scorpio, Water

CARCER: Prison, delay, entrapment, frustration, Capricorn, Earth

TRISTITIA: Sadness, loneliness, loss of a precious thing, Aquarius, Air

LAETITIA: Joy, laughter, health, good luck, Pisces, Water

CAUDA DRACONIS: An exit, you should leave now, Fire

CAPUT DRACONIS: A doorway, new beginning, stay on the path, Earth

FORTUNA MINOR: Lesser fortune, hard work, help from others, Leo, Water

VIA: The Way, travel, going it alone, a journey, Cancer, Water

Tasseomancy

TASSEOMANCY, OR tea-leaf reading, is one of the most iconic forms of divination. We've all seen images of a fortuneteller peering into a cup, seeing a client's future in the pattern of the leaves. Since tea, or coffee, is relatively cheap and can be found in most pantries, tasseomancy is one of the most widespread and accessible traditional ways of telling the future.

HISTORY

Romani fortune tellers are mostly credited with popularizing tasseomancy. As a nomadic people, they traveled from town to town across Europe and brought the practice with them. As the popularity of tea grew in Europe, so did tasseomancy as a form of divination. When coffee started to become more popular in the nineteenth and twentieth centuries, using coffee grounds to divine in a similar way became even more popular than tea-leaf reading, especially in countries like Greece and Turkey.

HOW-TO

Brew a cup (or pot) of loose-leaf tea by placing one teaspoon (get it?) of the tea of your choice in a mug and pouring in boiling hot water. If you are brewing a pot of tea for multiple people, add one scoop of tea per person and one "for the pot."

As the tea brews in your cup, begin to sip and either think about your question privately if you are alone, or converse with your client if you are reading for someone else. By the time you are done talking through the question or problem, you should be almost done with your tea and ready to divine.

When you are down to just a bit of water and the tea leaves left at the bottom of the cup, close your eyes, ask the question aloud, and flip the cup upside down onto a saucer or plate.

Then pick the cup back up, look inside, and try to associate images and symbols with the ways the leaves have stuck to the cup. Imagine as though you are a kid again and are looking up at the clouds to see what pictures you can make out. Don't overthink it.

Leaves that fall closer to the handle of the mug are things closer to you or the querent. Leaves on the opposite side of the mug are things outside you or the querent's sphere of influence. Leaves closer to the rim of the cup are events or things that might happen in the near future, while the bottom of the mug is the distant future.

TYPES OF TEA

Loose-leaf black tea is the most traditional type of tea used in tasseomancy, but you can use whatever herbs and spices you like to customize your divination practice. Below is a short list of herbs you can add to your tea, based on the properties they hold.

BASIL ★ Fire, money, wealth

CHAMOMILE ★ Water, peace, tranquility

CINNAMON ★ Fire, love, passion, warmth

CLOVE ★ Fire, passion, love

FENNEL ★ Fire, courage, strength

GINGER ★ Fire, passion, courage

LAVENDER ★ Air, love, peace, protection, psychic aid

MINT ★ Air, relaxation, aids in spirit work

MOTHERWORT ★ Air, peace, comfort, mood-soothing

MUGWORT ✳ Air, clairvoyance, dreams, aids in any divination work. (Do not use if pregnant.)

ROSEMARY ✳ Fire, protection, memory, boundaries

This book has been bound using handcraft methods and Smyth-sewn to ensure durability.

The cover and interior were illustrated by Sheyda Sabetian and designed by Celeste Joyce.